THE
LINKEDIN
MANUAL
FOR
ROOKIES

ANSWERING THAT AGE-OLD QUESTION:

Ok, I'm on LinkedIn . . .
Now What Do I Do?

DEBBIE MCCORMICK

Published by
Duswalt Press
280 N. Westlake Blvd
Westlake Village, CA 91362
Suite 110
www.duswaltpress.com

Manufactured in the United States of America, or in
the United Kingdom when distributed elsewhere.

Author: McCormick, Debbie
Title: The LinkedIn Manual For Rookies
ISBN:
Paperback: 9781938015502
eBook: 9781938015519

Cover design by: Joe Potter Design
Interior design: Scribe Inc.
Photo credits: Val Westover

Disclaimer:
Neither Debbie McCormick nor Debbie McCormick Consulting are
in any way associated with the LinkedIn Corporation.

Author's URL: www.McCormickConsulting.biz

Contents

Foreword

by Maryann Ehmann

With a membership of more than four hundred million, LinkedIn is one of those social media platforms that can increase your business or your frustrations—and quite possibly both. But let's face it, with too many frustrations, chances are you won't give LinkedIn the attention it requires in order to make it the useful tool it's designed to be.

Never fear! There is someone who can fix that for you so you can take full advantage of all this powerful platform has to offer.

Let me introduce you to Debbie McCormick, LinkedIn expert and writer. Debbie knows all too well the roadblocks, mishaps, and blunders so many have made on LinkedIn, as she has experienced them all herself. She understands how difficult it is to follow their "simple" directions, as well as implement best practices and strategies. Talk about hair pulling!

Not to be bested, Debbie grabbed the bull by the horns and made it her sole purpose in life to conquer this beast. After successfully doing so, it wasn't long before the word got out, and Debbie began helping many business owners and professionals tame LinkedIn and find their Ideal Clients with ease.

As a friend and mentor to Debbie, I have witnessed her work ethic, attention to detail, and bulldog tenacity to solve challenging problems, whether they are hers or others! She takes to heart the concerns of her clients and is brilliant at finding workable solutions. She has done just that with embracing the LinkedIn challenge, and now she brings it to you.

After much prompting from many believers, Debbie created this highly practical, step-by-step guide to attracting your Ideal Clients on LinkedIn, and she does it with great humor, clarity, and simplicity.

If you have been stymied by LinkedIn, aren't seeing results, wonder what the big deal is, or are stumped by how to maximize it, then get out of the fog and read Debbie McCormick's *LinkedIn Manual for Rookies*. Even if you have been on LinkedIn for years, take the time to reexamine your efforts, take her advice, and watch your client engagement soar!

Maryann Ehmann
Dream Activator and Business Strategist
Create Your Magnificent Lifestyle Business Now
http://createyourmagnificentlifestylebusiness.com

Acknowledgments

Thank you to everyone who encouraged me to write this book, especially the inaugural Leadership Launchpad gang. I'm proud to be one of you.

Two people in particular are responsible for implanting in my head the directive, "Get thee off thy tuchus and get this done . . . Now." Thank you so much, Craig Duswalt and Larry Broughton.

Maryann Ehmann, my Yoda: my appreciation for you is infinite. Thank you.

Huge thanks to:

Miriam Whiteley for your eagle eye and gift for the well-turned phrase.

Karen Strauss and Jason Hughes for shepherding me patiently through the publishing process.

Deborah Rachel Kagan for literally clearing the way.

Angela Rezzano, whose motto is always, "You'll be great!"

Sean McCormick and Gene Ehmann for your invaluable feedback and encouragement.

Edith Musgrove for your generosity and support, even now.

CHAPTER 1

Why I Wrote This Book

I've built my business on LinkedIn, and I love introducing people who can help each other's businesses there.

Why, you ask? What's so hot about LinkedIn?

Here's the deal:

- Cold-calling is dead. Social media now represents the greatest access to the people you want to do business with, your Ideal Clients. LinkedIn has proven to be the most effective social platform for business-to-business (B2B) lead generation—far more effective than Facebook or Twitter.

- The LinkedIn platform is designed to make it easy to connect. All the Fortune 1000 companies are represented there. LinkedIn gives you access to executives without having to cross the "secretary barrier."

- LinkedIn etiquette encourages long-term relationship building over pushy selling. The businesspeople who are successful on LinkedIn help their current and potential clients by providing them with useful information to help them succeed—without asking anything in return until they've earned the "ask," a concept (called Social Selling) that marketing guru Gary Vaynerchuk talks about all the time.
- It's easy to build your brand through an inviting profile, frequent posts, and participation in LinkedIn groups.

That's the good news.

The problem is that LinkedIn is not a quick or easy site to master. I won't tell you how many years my profile just sat there, unused, unloved, and forgotten because I didn't feel like I had the time to figure out to how to use it. (Okay, it was four years.) Yes, there are free tutorials, but honestly, I didn't think they were much help. So I gave up, just as many of you have.

Then I started reading everywhere how valuable LinkedIn was for doing business (at this writing, there are 128 million members in the United States alone and 433 million worldwide), so I thought I should probably give it another shot. This time, I read everything I could find on how to utilize LinkedIn to the fullest.

Then I discovered and came to love the concept of Social Selling, a relationship-building tool that is *perfect* to use on LinkedIn. But as I mastered Social Selling, I realized that until you know the basics of how to present your business on LinkedIn and how to practice its etiquette, all your Social Selling and marketing skills are as useless as stilettos on a bulldog.

That's why I wrote this book about LinkedIn fundamentals. When you're done reading, you'll have conquered the basics of LinkedIn, and it won't take you long. You'll soon be ready to utilize the principles of Social Selling (we'll get to that in chapter 15, "Fundamentals of Social Selling") to increase your prospects, clients, and income.

This book is perfect for you if you're interested in creating lasting business relationships based on providing exactly what your clients need. Whether you own your own business (or businesses), are rejoining the workforce, or have just graduated from college, if you want to learn or brush up on LinkedIn basics, you've found the right book. You'll learn how to:

- write a profile that draws your Ideal Clients to you
- connect with those clients in the proper way
- use LinkedIn etiquette

- customize your privacy settings
- lay the foundation for utilizing Social Selling and lead-generation techniques

You'll get the most out of this book if you start at the beginning and work your way through it in the order it's written (not necessarily in one sitting!).

Sometimes a picture is worth a thousand words, and a completed profile might be just the thing you need to see for clarity—please feel free to look over mine: http://www.LinkedIn.com/in/DebbieMcCormick.

The Hot Tips herein are denoted by the flame symbol 🔥.

Let's get this party started! Here's to your business success and prosperity on LinkedIn!

CHAPTER 2

Do You Really Need a Paid Membership?

You don't need a paid membership when you're just starting. LinkedIn's basic free membership is all that beginners need.

The biggest differences between the free and paid memberships are the availability of InMails (see chapter 19, "Introductions and InMails") and the number of Advanced Search filters (see chapter 23, "Search").

After we've gone through how to:

- write a powerful, engaging profile
- complete all the sections
- identify your Ideal Client
- write invitations that have the greatest chance of getting a positive response
- establish your privacy settings . . .

. . . then it'll be time to start thinking about how to find and reach out to that Ideal Client. Doing that may involve some of the Advanced Search options available only with a paid membership. You can decide at that time whether or not it's worth it to upgrade, which you can do at any time. (You can downgrade at any time too, but there are no prorated refunds. It's worth it to wait. That said, if you already have a Premium membership, please don't abandon it.)

If you haven't already, go to LinkedIn now and sign up for a free membership. Just follow the prompts: e-mail address, name, zip code, title, company, and so on. Upload your professional photo.

🔥 When you come to the "Finding Contacts" section, click *Deselect* and *Skip* all the way through it. LinkedIn will automatically send these contacts default connection requests, and we don't want to make connections just yet. I'll show you how to upload your contacts later in the book (see chapter 17, "Uploading Contacts").

CHAPTER 3

Don't Connect with Other Members . . . Yet

It may be fun to get on LinkedIn to see who you know, but at this beginning stage of building your profile, it's not in your best interest to connect with people—not yet. It's like going to a party without your pants on—not a good first impression.

Plus, and *this is really important*: there is an etiquette to connecting, both with those you know and especially with those you don't. You want to put your best professional self forward at all times, and how you connect goes a long way toward that. Or not.

So save the excitement for just a little bit. We'll put together a dynamite profile and learn how to connect properly, and *then* you can and should reach out to your heart's content.

CHAPTER 4

Profile Photograph: Go Pro

If a friend wanted to fix you up on a date with someone he or she thought would be perfect for you, would you want your friend to show that person a photo of your feet? Or the back of your head?

The correct answer would be no.

You'd hope your friend would show a photo of you at your best, wearing something you look great in, showing off all your best qualities.

The same principle applies on LinkedIn, except that this is a professional arena, and you now have the potential of being seen by literally millions. Not all of them are prospective clients, but you never know where the next referral will come from, right?

So the smart money says you should have your photo taken by a pro. This is the person who will light you correctly, feature your best side, and make sure you have a single chin with a clean jawline.

Dress professionally.

It's not only the pose that's important; the finishing touches are also crucial. You don't have to post a photo showing all your blotches and puffy eyes in the name of authenticity. Let a pro clean you up for the spotlight—your profile photo is the first impression a LinkedIn member will have of you. Make it a great one.

Going to a pro doesn't have to be expensive. Do some homework: Groupon, the local university for photography students, your chamber of commerce, Yelp.

My first LinkedIn photos were taken by someone who had just turned his photography hobby into his full-time business, so he was happy to charge a smaller-than-average fee to help him build his clientele. I knew his work, was confident he knew his stuff, and I loved the pics.

Under-eye circles? What under-eye circles?

CHAPTER 5

The "Notify Your Network" Setting

We're going to do the lion's share of choosing your settings later on, but there's one that's important to turn off now and keep off forever, especially if you've already made some connections.

It's called the "Notify Your Network" setting and refers to whether or not you want your connections to be notified every time you change anything—even a comma—on your profile. Being on the receiving end of that can get annoying fast, so let's just shut this off.

1. Go up to the navigation bar at the top of any page. (Notice that when the navigation bar is hidden, you can hover over the bar area, and it will appear. It's magic.)

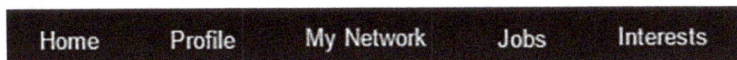

Home	Profile	My Network	Jobs	Interests

2. Click Profile or Edit Profile.
3. Scroll down a little, and on the right side of the page, you'll see a box that says "Notify Your Network?" and a button that you can slide. Slide it to *No*.

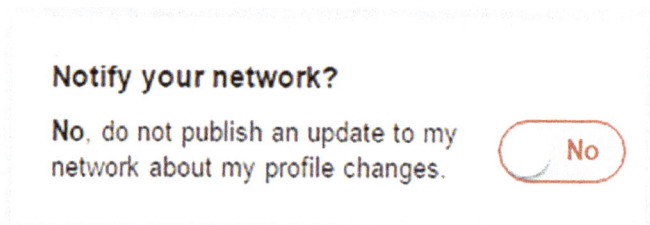

Notify your network?

No, do not publish an update to my network about my profile changes.

No

Every so often, glance over to that box when you're in Edit mode and make sure that button still says No. I noticed that mine had shifted to Yes even though I hadn't changed it, so keep your eye on it.

CHAPTER 6

Write All Sections Offline

This tip alone is going to save you much time and many headaches. Write *everything* in a word processing app *before* you post anything on LinkedIn. Here's why.

First, you can't hide your profile from other members. You can hide it from the public, but not from other members doing searches or just happening upon it.

Second, you don't want your profile to look half-dressed, with some sections written and some not, no profile photo, and so on. If it looks sloppy, readers will think you're sloppy, and that's not what you want.

I suggest following the steps in this order:

1. Become a member with a basic membership.
2. Deselect any options to connect with or notify contacts that you're now on LinkedIn (see chapter 2, "Do You Really Need A Paid Membership?"

3. Put up a great, professionally done photo.
4. Fill out your name, headline (more about how to write an excellent headline later; for now, just put your job title), and industry. Leave everything else blank.

Now you have two things going for you:

1. When someone comes across your profile, it'll look neat and clean, even though it's incomplete.
2. Now you'll be able to see all the sections that you have the opportunity to complete and what prompts each gives you. As you get each section written in your word processing app, you can see what you need to do next.

When you do all your writing in your word processor, you can take your time and edit it for as long as you like. Once you post your writing on your profile page, LinkedIn saves it, so if you post one section at a time, it has that half-baked look. Better to post all your sections in the same sitting, so that when you're done, you have a complete and shiny new profile.

CHAPTER 7

Who Is Your Ideal Client?

Identifying your Ideal Client is not just a great idea for LinkedIn—it's a marketing necessity.

Who is the perfect client for your business? That's your Ideal Client (IC), and that's who you want to have in mind when you're writing your profile Summary and Experiences.

To begin, I went through a checklist:

- gender
- employment status
- income
- company position or title
- industry
- education status
- age

So, for example, the perfect client for my services would be someone who is interested in creating or furthering her business relationships through LinkedIn—whether she's already in business, transitioning into the workplace, or a recent college grad—but doesn't know how to use LinkedIn and doesn't feel like she can take the time necessary to teach herself. It doesn't matter what age or gender she is, or what her business experience is, as long as she wants to learn or brush up on the fundamentals of LinkedIn. Voilà, my IC.

Identifying your IC helps you in many ways, mainly in giving you a focus for your communications. I found it hugely useful to picture a real person, one of my favorite clients, and write to her. Every article I write is with her in mind: what can I teach or explain to her about LinkedIn or marketing that will help her with her business? If I feel I've accomplished that, it's a good article.

CHAPTER 8

Profile Headline: Keywords Are Vital

Your headline is the other "first" impression a reader will have of you—readers will see either your headline or your photo first.

Here's the insider secret about profile headlines that most people don't know: you must use your keywords.

> 🔥 Keywords are just search terms. If someone wanted to find you, what words would she or he type into a search engine? Those are your keywords.

Using your keywords in your profile headline assists the LinkedIn search engine in finding you.

As an example, here is my profile headline:

- LinkedIn Trainer
- Lead Generation and Social Selling Specialist
- LinkedIn Fundamentals Coach

See how those terms are exactly what someone who is looking for a LinkedIn coach or trainer would type into a search engine? The headline incorporates my most important keywords: trainer, lead generation, Social Selling, fundamentals, and coach.

> 🔥 Searchers on LinkedIn most often search by using personal terms instead of job titles, so you want your keywords to reflect that. For example, on LinkedIn I use the keyword "trainer" (who I am) instead of "LinkedIn training" (what I do).

CHAPTER 9

Profile Summary

If Your Bio and Résumé Had a Child

Under your photo, you'll see the words "Add a section to your profile" and, just under that, "View More." Click View More and you'll see all the sections available for you to complete. We'll go through each of these sections.

Here are some good tips for the Summary section.

Think of the LinkedIn Summary as the child of a bio and a résumé, with one big twist: you need to write it with your Ideal Client (IC) in mind, answering the two questions your IC wants to know:

1. Am I in the right place (reading the right profile)?
2. What can this person do to solve my problem(s)?

As suggested earlier, pick a real person who embodies all the characteristics of your IC. Write to this person about how you got started, what you offer, and who you work with, as follows.

I've included my Summary so you can easily see an example.

Summary Part 1

Start your Summary with a paragraph explaining how you got to this point in your business life. How did you get into your business, what were the inspirations that launched you in this direction—that kind of thing. I included exactly how I want to be of service to my clients:

My goal is to increase my clients' business successes by teaching them insider tips and tricks to take full advantage of every level of LinkedIn. I am committed to my high standard of excellence, integrity, and service.

A few years ago, I found it frustrating that LinkedIn was so difficult to intuitively understand and use. If you too have felt that way, I get it. I learned LinkedIn from top to bottom, and now I teach all the little tricks I gathered to make your time on LinkedIn successful and productive.

I will teach you how to easily showcase your expertise, increase your credibility, reach out to your target audience, and generate business leads using LinkedIn.

Summary Part 2

You can list your specialties before or after your types of clientele, whichever you prefer. I did clientele first, because my primary goal is to have the reader recognize him- or herself as someone I specialize in working with.

Highlight for the reader the kinds of people you work with by listing their job titles. This helps answer question #1 above ("Am I in the right place?") at a glance.

CLIENTELE:
♦ *Business Owners/Entrepreneurs*
♦ *Senior Executives*
♦ *Marketing Professionals*
♦ *General Managers*
♦ *Real Estate Professionals*
♦ *Professionals in Career Transition*
♦ *Recent College Graduates*

Summary Part 3

Tell the reader exactly what you offer. Even if she's not looking for one of the services you've listed, she may feel that what she needs is close enough to what you offer that she'll at least reach out to you to discuss her needs—which is exactly what you want.

SPECIALTIES:
- ★ *Using LinkedIn to build your business and brand*
- ★ *Optimum keyword usage and placement*
- ★ *How to stand out on LinkedIn*
- ★ *LinkedIn lead generation*
- ★ *Social Selling on LinkedIn*

Summary Part 4

Include all your contact info and a call to action (for example, "Contact me today."). You'll be doing this in a few different places throughout your profile, because people don't always read from the top straight through to the bottom. They skip around, they're in a hurry— just like you sometimes are when you're online. You want the reader to easily find how to reach you so she doesn't have to search and possibly give up.

CONTACT me today to start increasing your business through LinkedIn:
- ► *Send me a PERSONALIZED (please) LinkedIn connection request*
- ► *E-mail me today*: Debbie@McCormickConsulting .BIZ

► *Read more about the services I offer at* http://www .McCormickConsulting.BIZ

Within the Summary section, as in many others, you may add media, like company videos, documents, presentations, work samples, and photos to further illustrate how you can be of service to potential clients.

That's it! You'll have a well-organized Summary that's a pleasure to read and that tells your potential client exactly what she needs to know to decide if she wants to pursue you and your services/products further.

Debbie's Summary Example in Full

My goal is to increase my clients' business success by teaching them insider tips and tricks to take full advantage of every level of LinkedIn. I am committed to my high standard of excellence, integrity, and service.

A few years ago, I found it frustrating that LinkedIn was so difficult to intuitively understand and use. If you too have felt that way, I get it. I learned LinkedIn from top to bottom, and now I teach other professionals all the little tricks I gathered to make your time on LinkedIn successful and productive.

☛ *I will teach you how to easily showcase your expertise, increase your credibility, reach out to your target audience, and generate business leads using LinkedIn.* ☚

CLIENTELE:
♦ *Business Owners/Entrepreneurs*
♦ *Senior Executives*
♦ *Marketing Professionals*
♦ *General Managers*
♦ *Real Estate Professionals*
♦ *Professionals in Career Transition*
♦ *Recent College Graduates*

SPECIALTIES:
★ *Using LinkedIn to build your business and brand*
★ *Optimum keyword usage and placement*
★ *How to stand out on LinkedIn*
★ *LinkedIn lead generation*
★ *Social Selling on LinkedIn*

CONTACT *me today to start increasing your business through LinkedIn*:
► *Send me a PERSONALIZED (please) LinkedIn connection request*
► *E-mail me today*: Debbie@McCormickConsulting.BIZ

▶ *Read more about the services I offer at* http://www .McCormickConsulting.BIZ

🔥 If you'd like to add symbols to your profile after you've posted it, go to a profile on the site that has them (like mine), then copy and paste. LinkedIn continually changes which symbols they allow to be pasted, so just play with it and have some fun.

CHAPTER 10

Work Experience

Describe the jobs you've held from the most recent to the earliest, giving about ten years' worth of information. Don't just list the tasks you were responsible for, but rather discuss how you positively affected the company.

For example, "Jill" could say that she was responsible for monthly inventory and leave it at that. What would be more beneficial to her (and helpful to a potential employer thinking of stealing her away) is if she wrote instead that in being responsible for monthly inventory, she saved her company thousands of dollars by changing the inventory process to a simpler and faster system.

> 🔥 Tell how the tasks you performed in your job positively impacted the company: saved time, saved money, or both. In other words, how did you serve the company?

If you're looking to change careers, emphasize any previous experiences that will help you hit the ground running in your new field—the ways you can positively impact your new company as you have working for your previous employers.

CHAPTER 11

The Remaining Sections

To finish the rest of your profile, we'll go back to the top of your profile page. Your goal here is to complete all the sections that are relevant to you.

Contact Info
Under your large photo, you'll see a little button that says "Contact Info." Click to find the contact information you can make available for your first-degree connections to see.

First, fill in your email and business phone. If you work from your home and don't see clients there, leave your address blank. If you want prospective clients to initially contact you only by email, leave your phone number blank. Otherwise, put your business phone number there and your instant messaging information if you like.

If you have a Twitter account for your business, enter your Twitter name without the "@" symbol.

Since you always want to customize your profile and communications instead of using LinkedIn's default wording, take advantage of being able to do that with your business website. Instead of leaving the label as Company Website, click Other to customize your website's name. Then fill in the URL. Do that with any other contact information you're allowed to customize.

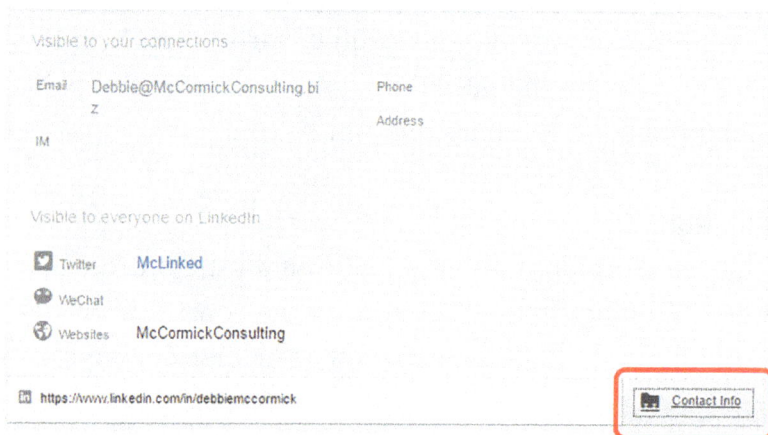

Visible to your connections

Email   Debbie@McCormickConsulting.biz   Phone

IM   Address

Visible to everyone on LinkedIn

Twitter   McLinked

WeChat

Websites   McCormickConsulting

https://www.linkedin.com/in/debbiemccormick   Contact Info

Skills and Endorsements

Here you may add the skills you've become known for (or would like to be known for), and anyone—even people who don't know you—can endorse you for them. (Takes a little of the value out of them, doesn't it?) You may control which skills are shown if someone add skills that don't fit what you're doing now.

Education

Fill out as much as you're comfortable with. You don't have to have graduated from college to list having attended. You don't need to put the dates you attended, especially if you're an older worker coming back into the workforce. If you didn't go to college, you may leave it blank or list your high school.

> 🔥 As you've no doubt heard many times, we do business with people we:
>
> _know_   _like_   _trust_
>
> Several of the upcoming sections are designed to let the reader get to know you a little better as a person for just that reason.

Volunteer

If you have a favorite cause or organization you volunteer for, include those details here.

Causes You Care About and Organizations You Support

LinkedIn gives you categories of interests, plus you can add your own.

Interests

Anything you like can go here: sports, hobbies, books you like, and so on.

Advice for Contacting You

This is another opportunity to let people know how they can reach you, so include e-mail, website, phone, and address as appropriate.

Courses, Organizations, Certifications, Patents, Honors, Projects, and So On

Fill out the rest of the sections that pertain to you. If you don't have any patents, for instance, or don't speak a second language, just leave those areas blank.

🔥 LinkedIn rewards you for your profile completeness by giving you a rating that only you can see when you are in Edit Profile mode. It's over on the right side of the page, called Profile Strength. Your goal is to be an All-Star, meaning your profile is complete.

Profile Strength

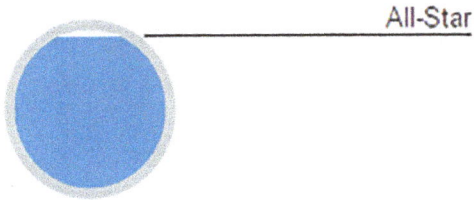

All-Star

CHAPTER 12

Background Photo

At the top of your profile page when you're in Edit mode, you'll see the words "Add Background Photo."

The background photo is an area where you can show what you do—show a photo of a book you've written, a photo of you speaking in public . . . anything that highlights your work.

LinkedIn gives the following parameters for this image:

- jpg, png, or gif
- under 8 MB in size
- 1400 × 425 pixels

I found I had to play with the size a little, but it didn't take long to get it right. I used a graphic designer to get the sharpest possible jpg image.

CHAPTER 13

Profile Privacy Settings

Just between you and me, this isn't the most fun part of setting up your profile. It's necessary, though, so that your profile is presented the way you want it to be, both to LinkedIn members and to the public. Promise yourself a good treat afterward, like chocolate ice cream or an adult beverage.

Those settings that are self-explanatory, I'll skip. Some do need greater explanation than LinkedIn provides, so here we go.

Hover over your thumbnail photo in the upper-right corner, then click Privacy and Settings on the drop-down menu.

Account Settings/Basics
You'll automatically land on your Account Settings/ Basics page. Enter your e-mail address and your phone

number (this is for LinkedIn's administrative benefit and will not show on your profile unless you specifically enter it under Contact Info). This is also where you can change your password.

You'll be given some choices as to how you want your location and industry to read.

If you decide to embed videos in your profile, this is where you can choose whether they start to play the moment someone opens your profile.

Showing Profile Photos

This refers to showing photos of other members. For example, in your status feed (see chapter 21, "Status Updates"), you could choose not to show the photos of the people whose posts you see. But why wouldn't you want to see them? I can't think of a good reason not to, so choose Everyone. You can change it at any time.

Third-Party Apps

The only third party that has access to my LinkedIn account is LinkedIn Help.

Twitter settings allow you to choose whether you automatically and simultaneously post your LinkedIn posts to your Twitter business account. Same with WeChat.

The remainder of the Account Settings are straightforward.

Privacy Settings

Click on Privacy in the center of the page, and you'll see that the first thing you can edit is your public profile.

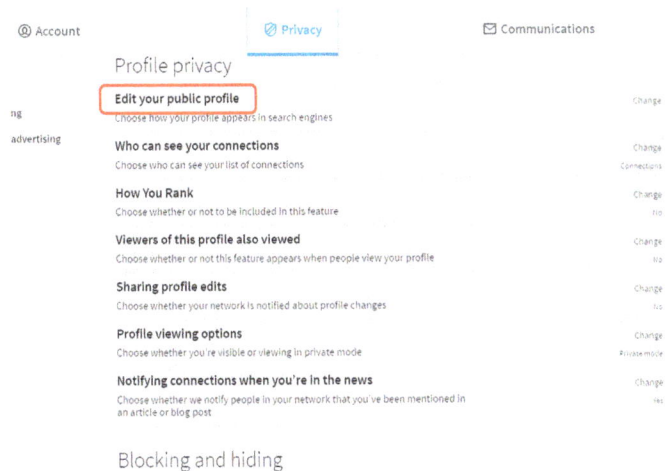

Editing Your Public Profile

When someone Googles you, one of the first results that will appear is your LinkedIn profile. The public profile section is where you can determine what that person sees as opposed to what LinkedIn members see from inside LinkedIn.

> 🔥 The "public" is defined here as anyone who isn't a LinkedIn member.

First, decide if you even want your LinkedIn profile to be visible to search engines. I don't know of any good reason you wouldn't; the whole point of being on LinkedIn is to market yourself and your business; being available to search engines just broadens that reach. Also, because LinkedIn is such a large platform, your LinkedIn profile will come up near or at the top of any search for you.

Customize Your Public Profile

Control how you appear when people search for you on Google, Yahoo, Bing, etc.
Learn more ›

○ Make my public profile visible to no one
● Make my public profile visible to everyone

Basics
☑ Picture
☑ Headline
☑ Websites
☑ Posts
☑ Summary
☑ Current Positions
  ☑ Details
☐ Past Positions
☐ Skills
☑ Education
  ☑ Details
☐ Volunteer Experiences & Causes
☐ Interests
☐ Publications
☐ Courses
☐ Certifications
☑ Recommendations
☐ Groups

If you'd like the public to be able to see everything that LinkedIn members see, just check all the boxes.

My goal for people who are interested in me and my business is to have them join me on LinkedIn (it's free, after all), where I have more access to them and they to me. To help them choose to do that, I show only my posts, Summary, current job, education, and recommendations in my public profile. The interests, volunteer experiences, and so on—those I save for members of LinkedIn. There is no right or wrong way to do it, so choose what makes sense to you.

Customize Your LinkedIn URL

Your LinkedIn public profile has its own unique URL, which you can customize; find it just above the "Customize Your Public Profile" area on the right side of the page, in the upper-right corner. LinkedIn will have assigned you some random numbers at the end of the general LinkedIn URL. Click the blue pencil icon, and you'll see how you can customize the address.

Your public profile URL

Enhance your personal brand by creating a custom URL for your LinkedIn public profile.

www.linkedin.com/in/debbiemccormick

Use your personal name, not your business name. If you have a common name that has already been taken, you'll need to add a middle initial or a number at the end of your name to make it uniquely yours.

Choose Who Can See Your Connections

There are two schools of thought on this setting. The reason to show your connections is so they can see each other—the whole point of networking. Your connections who would like to explore doing business together might ask you for an introduction (see chapter 20, "Introductions and InMails").

The reason not to show them is to prevent your competitors from contacting those connections they think are clients and trying to steal them.

One of my main purposes for being on LinkedIn is to introduce my connections to each other so they can do business together. And I make sure my clients receive more value than they pay for, so I'm comfortable letting people see my connections.

Viewers of This Profile Also Viewed

I don't recommend that you turn on this setting. When this is on, a reader of your profile can see which other profiles your previous readers have viewed . . . in other words, your competition. Why give those folks a show-case on *your* profile?

Profile-Viewing Options

Here you can choose whether to reveal who you are when you view other people's profiles. The only reason I can think of to choose Anonymous is when you're viewing your competition's profile and you don't want him to know you're looking at him. That's perfectly legit. Ordinarily, let people see that you're looking at them. You may get a message in response and start a dialogue beneficial to both of you.

Blocking and Hiding

You may block anyone who is exhibiting disturbing behavior, like stalking or sending you inappropriate messages, or someone you would rather not hear from for any reason.

CHAPTER 14

Posting Your Profile

Congratulations! If you've followed this book's sections in order, you're now done writing your profile! Great job!

Now it's time to post it. Set aside a couple hours to do this, because posting an entire profile to LinkedIn never seems to go flawlessly. You want to post from beginning to end, all in one sitting, so that when you're done it's complete and looks gorgeous. Leaving it half-done looks unprofessional. (And be sure to reward yourself afterward.)

Start at the top with your profile headline and work down, cutting from your word processor and pasting into each section. Upload your professional photo and any media. Remember to click Save at the end of each section.

CHAPTER 15

Fundamentals of Social Selling

Don't let the word *selling* fool you—social selling is also about smart marketing, and LinkedIn is one of the platforms on which it's most effective.

Social Selling is about learning what your clients need, then sharing information that will positively impact their businesses before you ever ask for the sale. "Give, give, give, ask," is how Gary Vaynerchuk and other marketing experts put it. You *earn* the ask. Let me show you how I do it as an example.

I publish regularly on LinkedIn and Twitter (@McLinked) about LinkedIn's best practices, and on my website you can download my free PDF, *12 Hot Tips to Increase Your Business on LinkedIn*.

That's Social Selling. Give, give, give. In other words: clarify, educate, enlighten—then you've earned their business.

> 🔥 To further your business relationship, take your conversation offline by requesting a telephone or face-to-face appointment.

CHAPTER 16

LinkedIn Etiquette

Using the Social Selling model is part of the etiquette that works so well on LinkedIn because everything you do and write is personal and directed toward serving your clients.

Connections and Contacts

A *contact* is someone you've uploaded from your address book. You can upload contacts using the navigation bar at the top of your page, under My Network.

Home	Profile	My Network	Jobs	Interests

A *contact* becomes a *connection* when that person has accepted your connection request or you have accepted his or hers. In other words, a connection has to be one of your contacts, but a contact isn't necessarily a connection.

Connection Requests

The mistake I see most often on LinkedIn is people sending connection requests using LinkedIn's default wording. It goes like this:

"Hi Debbie, I'd like to add you to my professional network on LinkedIn."

Yawn.

The two things I don't like about this generic, boring message . . . other than the fact that it's generic and boring . . . are:

1. If I know the writer, I would love for her to personalize her message to really catch my attention, like, "Hey girl! Long time, no see! How ya doing? Let's connect!"
2. If I don't know the writer, it's even more important that it be personalized. Why did the writer reach out to me? Have we met? Where? How does she know of me?

When reaching out to someone you don't know, use these suggestions to personalize the request:

- Though you'll be offered the opportunity to connect with others in many areas of the site, <u>always connect from the individual's profile</u>. That way, you'll always have the opportunity to customize the message. Other areas, such as Search and Uploading Contacts, don't give you that important opportunity.
- Use a warm, conversational tone, and write the way you talk.
- Tell him how you know of him: *I read your article about marketing in Inc. magazine.* Or, *I heard you speak at the ABC Marketing Seminar.*
- Or where you met: *We were introduced at the ABC Marketing Seminar.*
- Or remark on something in his profile: *I see we both have a passion for UNICEF.*
- Give feedback: *Your suggestion of a daily marketing to-do list inspired me to make one immediately.*
- Then the connection request: *I would like to keep up with you and would be very happy to have you in my LinkedIn network.*

Send appealing invitations that are heartfelt and personalized, and I guarantee you'll experience a lot more acceptances than rejections.

> 🔥 *Always* customize your LinkedIn communications so that your messages and requests are personal. Never use LinkedIn's default wording; it looks like you were too lazy to make the note special.

Should You Connect with Everyone Who Asks?
No. Avoid connecting with:

- people whose profiles look sketchy—that is, no info or photo
- people who send you requests from across the continent or from a foreign country if you are a merchant whose clientele is local

Consider this: though someone who asks to connect may not be your Ideal Client, he or she may know someone in need of your services. Be thoughtful about your connections, but don't automatically rule them out just because they're not direct clients for your services.

CHAPTER 17

Uploading Contacts

Ominous warning: There is a tricky step here, so stay with the instructions so you don't make a mistake you can't take back.

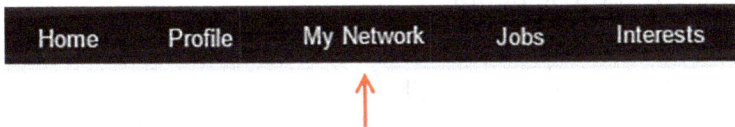

First, go up to the top of the page to your navigation bar and click My Network, then Add Contacts.

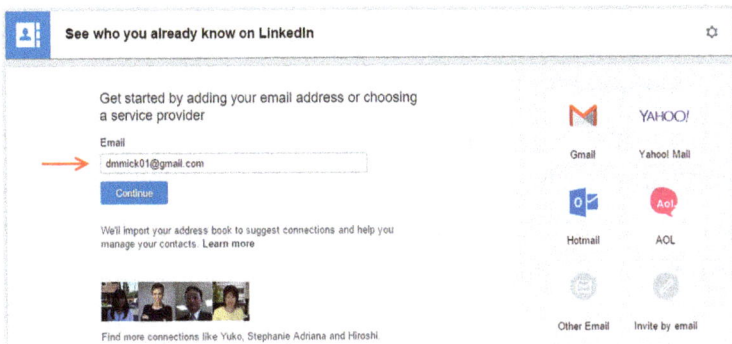

Enter your e-mail address where indicated, and LinkedIn will show you everyone in your address book who is already on LinkedIn.

Here's the tricky part:

Do not click Add Connections at the top of the page.

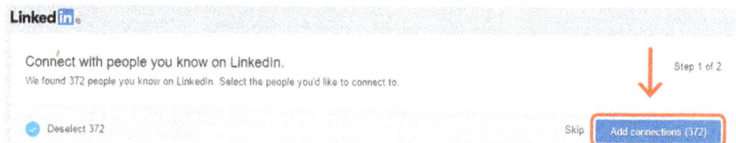

Whew, that was close.

If you push that blue Add Connections button, LinkedIn's boring default connection request will go out to all those people.

Instead, look to the left of the rectangle to find the Deselect option and click that.

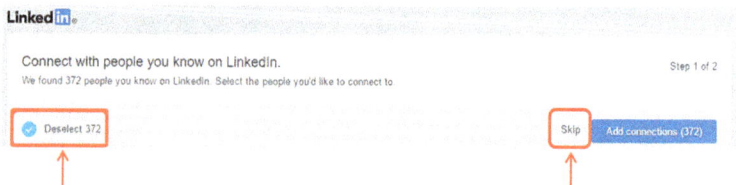

Then click Skip.

The next page you land on will show the people in your address book who are not yet on LinkedIn. If you push the Add to Network button, again at the top of the page, all these nice folks will get an e-mail from

LinkedIn saying that they should join you on the site. And they'll be nagged up to two more times if they don't join immediately. Good way to irritate your friends.

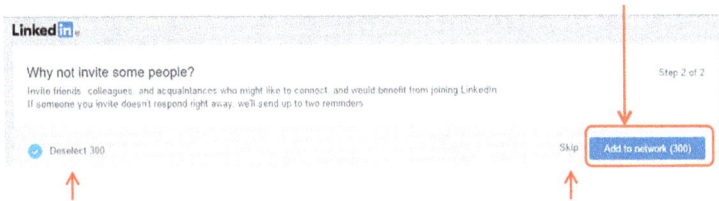

Again, choose Deselect, then Skip.

You'll then land on a page called "People You May Know." If you see people with whom you'd like to connect, <u>click on their names to go to their profiles and connect there, not on the People You May Know page</u>. Again, don't take the chance that you won't be able to personalize the message.

It may sound like a lot of extra work to choose one person at a time to write them an individualized note, but it will pay off big time in the long run.

CHAPTER 18

Understanding Connections

Your Sphere of Influence

LinkedIn makes it easy to connect with other members.

First-Degree Connection

When you reach out to someone, inviting him or her to connect, and he or she accepts your invitation, you have established a first-degree connection directly between you and someone else. That's also true when someone reaches out to you.

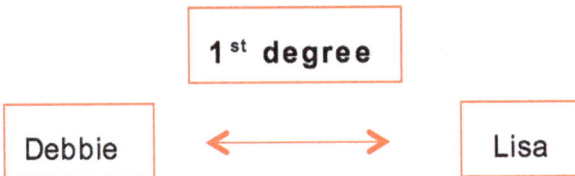

1ˢᵗ degree

Debbie ← → Lisa

Second-Degree Connection

When Lisa invites someone to become her first-degree connection, that person becomes my second-degree connection. This connection is indirect; I may not know Joe. I am a second-degree connection to all Lisa's first-degree, or direct, connections. And that's true with every first-degree connection you have! The more quality first-degree connections you have, the more exponentially your business universe grows. (See "The Power of Second-Degree Connections" in this chapter.)

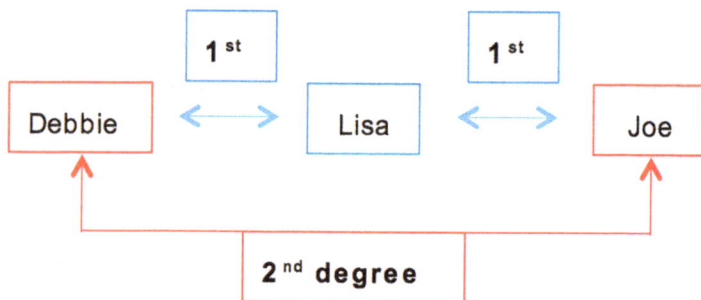

If I reached out to Joe, invited him to connect directly, and he accepted my invitation, he would become one of my first-degree connections. Lisa, Joe, and I would all be directly connected with each other.

Third-Degree Connection

You already know what's coming:

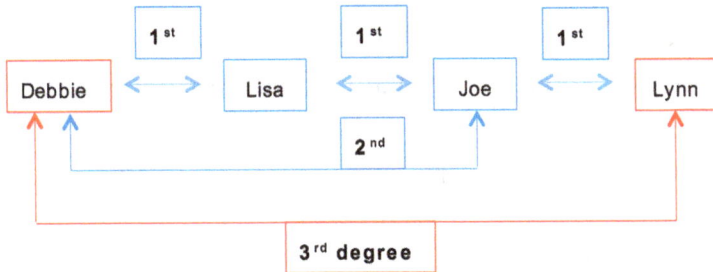

The Power of Second-Degree Connections

Second-degree connections are highly valuable because, though you may not know them, they're people with whom you have at least one connection in common, like Joe and I have Lisa in common in the above example. That makes it much easier for you to be introduced or to introduce yourself to them if they fit the profile of your Ideal Client.

In the next chapter, "Introductions and InMails," you'll learn how to ask a common connection (i.e., Lisa) to introduce you to your second-degree connection (Joe). The great thing about getting introduced to Joe by Lisa is that Joe already knows Lisa, so you're not coming in out of the blue. The hang-up there: if Joe and Lisa actually don't know each other; you'll have to check with Lisa before you request an intro. If that's the case, you might as well introduce yourself to Joe directly.

If Joe's profile allows you to, send him a connection request—personalized, of course—saying that you both know Lisa and explaining why you'd like to connect with him.

The more you introduce yourself to your second-degree connections and become directly connected to them, the bigger your network of people to whom you can be of service grows.

CHAPTER 19

Introductions and InMails

When you'd like to reach out to someone you don't know, you may do it in one of three ways:

- Send her a connection request (see the section on "Connection Requests" in chapter 16, "LinkedIn Etiquette").
- Send her an InMail (only available if you have a Premium membership) if you don't know her e-mail.
- Ask for an introduction if you are a second-degree connection of hers.

Introductions

An introduction is made by someone who knows both you and the person you want to meet; in other words, one of your first-degree connections.

In the example in the "Connection Requests" section above, I am a second-degree connection with Joe. If I wanted to be directly connected to him—a first-degree connection—I could send him a <u>personalized</u> connection request mentioning that we both know Lisa and telling him why I'd like to be connected with him.

Another way I could do it would be to reach out to Lisa and ask for what's called a "warm" introduction to Joe, meaning an intro from someone he knows. Before doing that, I would contact Lisa to make sure she actually knows Joe and is okay with making the introduction.

If she is, and Joe and Lisa do know each other, I'll go to Joe's profile. To the right of his name, I'll see "2nd," confirming that he and I are second-degree connections.

Scrolling down and looking at the right side of the page, I come to the "How you're connected" section and see Lisa's photo, since that's who Joe and I both know. Directly under Lisa's photo, I find a link that says "Ask Lisa for an introduction."

After clicking the link, I'm taken to my messages page. In the center of the page is a dialog box that says, "Lisa, can you introduce me to Joe?" or "Request an intro" or very similar wording, depending on the type of account you have.

Remember: Never send LinkedIn's default message.

🔥 When writing the request for an intro message to your direct connection, Lisa, keep in mind that Lisa may forward your request for an intro directly to Joe without adding anything to it. So write the message to Lisa as if that's the case. For example, "Lisa, would you please introduce me to Joe Shmoe? He uses a product very similar to mine in his business, and I'd like to introduce myself." This way, if Lisa does pass it on verbatim, Joe will know why you want to meet him.

The only problem with requesting an introduction is that Lisa may be so busy that she forgets to send a request to Joe or to even forward the request you sent to her. In other words, there's no guarantee that Joe will see or hear of your request.

You don't have that problem when sending InMails.

InMail

You may send an InMail to any member you're not connected to, but only if you have a Premium (paid) membership.

For those who do have a Premium membership, depending on your kind of subscription, you are allowed "X" number of free InMails per month. If you want to use more than your allotted amount, you can buy up to ten more.

To see how many you have, hover over your thumbnail photo, then click Account. That information will be on the right side of the page.

If you're in the market for a job, InMails are great for reaching out to potential employers. In chapter 24, "Search," you'll learn how to find the profiles of managers and executives at the companies you want to work for.

Look for the blue rectangle just below the profile headline. It may say read "Send X InMail," as in the example below, or you might need to click on the down arrow in that rectangle to find the Send InMail option.

As with all your LinkedIn communications, make this a warm, personable, *concise* introduction of yourself and your reason for contacting this person. Before writing, determine your desired outcome or goal. Do you want to connect with her on LinkedIn (you would need to send a connection request separate from the InMail), or request a meeting or phone call? Have your goal in mind as you write.

If you don't receive an answer to your InMail within a certain amount of time, LinkedIn will credit you for it.

Messaging

A message is just an e-mail that you may send to your connections and contacts directly from:

- the LinkedIn messaging page, accessed from the upper-right corner

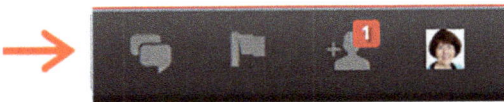

- your Contacts page (found in the navigation bar at the top of the page under My Network)

Home	Profile	My Network	Jobs	Interests

- their profile page under their large photo

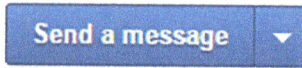

Send a message ▼

CHAPTER 20

Status Updates

Your status area is on the left side of your Home page (see the navigation bar at the top of any page).

Here you can see what your connections have recently posted.

When you update your status, share information that is helpful, educational, and enlightening. It can be anything from sharing an inspirational quote, to something that's trending on LinkedIn, to how something in the news will impact business. Just keep it business oriented.

I see many realtors make the mistake of putting their listings in their Status Updates. A realtor's listing in Anaheim Hills, California, for example, is going to be of interest to very few of LinkedIn's millions of readers.

If instead he posted, for instance, that the *Los Angeles Times* had just reported that the Fed was thinking of dropping interest rates, that would be interesting news to buyers and sellers, as well as other realtors all over the country. Other realtors, to continue the example, will realize that this guy is on top of things and refer their business to him when they have a buyer in his county. Locals, both realtors and the public, will start to follow him on LinkedIn, Twitter, and other social media for the same reason.

Share without asking anything in return, and watch your reputation grow.

> 🔥 It is inappropriate to sell your wares in your status posts. Share, educate, inspire, and inform. Do not sell.

CHAPTER 21

Recommendations

Receiving recommendations of your work is invaluable on LinkedIn. It's like getting five stars on Amazon.

You may give and receive recommendations with only your first-degree connections. You may request as many recommendations as you like, and you get to choose which are displayed and in what order.

To request or give a recommendation, go to that person's profile page and click the arrow of the blue rectangle to the right of the person's profile photo.

Click Recommend, and you'll land on the Recommendations page. There you may give or request a recommendation, plus see from whom you've requested one and to whom you've given one.

I've included the "Write a recommendation" form for you to see. It's just fill-in-the-blank.

If you receive a recommendation and it contains errors, for instance spelling your name incorrectly, you may send it back to the writer requesting a change. Be gentle. After all, you want the recommendation to reflect well on your client as well as on your work.

Recommendations are very different from endorsements, mainly in that recommendations can only be given by your first-degree connections. Endorsements may be given by any member, even if they don't know you. (Kind of shaves some of the credibility off of endorsements, doesn't it?)

1 **Write a recommendation**

If needed, you can make changes or delete it even after you send it.

> Ex. Lisa is very detail-oriented and produced great results for the company.

Your message to Lisa

You can personalize this message if you'd like.

> Hi Lisa,
> I wrote this recommendation of your work that you can include on your profile.
> Thanks,
> Debbie
> http://www.linkedin.com/recs/received

2 **What's your relationship?**

> Choose...

What were your positions at the time?

You: Choose...

Lisa: Choose...

Send   Cancel

70

CHAPTER 22

Groups

Groups are formed around a common industry, job, or interest. They are private, and you will see the conversations taking place within a group only after you are a member. After choosing a group, click the Ask to Join button on the right side of the group's page. The group's administrator or founder decides who joins and can also issue invitations to join.

The administrator can remove conversations that don't pertain to the group's purpose, and other members can flag conversations as inappropriate. One of the quickest ways to be removed from a group is to post sales pitches.

If you've been accepted into a group about marketing, for example, you could ask for marketing advice or advise someone else who has asked a question, establishing yourself as an expert and thought leader.

To find groups of interest to you, go to the search box at the top of every page (see chapter 24, "Search"). Click the left menu, choose Groups, then type keywords for the group or its name in the search box.

Or you can click on Interests in the navigation bar at the top of any page and choose Groups. You'll land on a page that lists the groups to which you already belong. At the top of that page, click Discover to see which groups LinkedIn recommends for you based on the keywords in your profile.

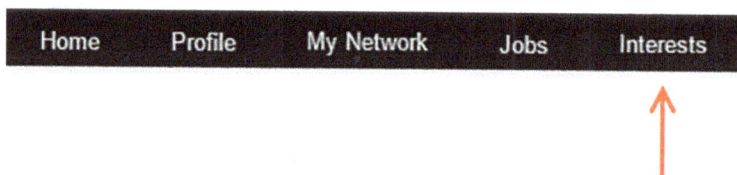

You may become a member of up to 50 groups. While you can certainly choose groups reflecting your personal interests, keep the majority of the ones you join about business, preferably those in which you can answer questions, give advice, and show your expertise on the subject.

CHAPTER 23

Search

Basic and Advanced Search are two of the best features on LinkedIn, in my humble opinion. You can find *anyone*, and most members give you some way to reach out to them.

I say "most" because there are some to whom you can't even send an InMail—you must know their e-mail addresses. One example is Bill Gates of Microsoft fame. You can follow him, which will allow his posts to appear in your Status Updates. But if you want to reach out to him, you have to know his e-mail address. He doesn't allow InMail, messages, or connections.

Basic Search

The Search box is in the middle at the top of every page.

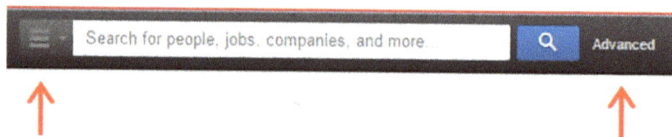

The menu on the left of the box narrows your search categories into the following:

- People
- Jobs
- Companies
- Groups
- Universities
- Posts
- Inbox

Advanced Search

Click Advanced on the right of the box, and you'll land on the Advanced Search page, which gives you even more categories with which to narrow your search.

Look at all the *free* search filters you have access to!

The categories on the right with the gold "in" squares are those you can utilize as a paid member; which categories you can use depends on the kind of membership you have.

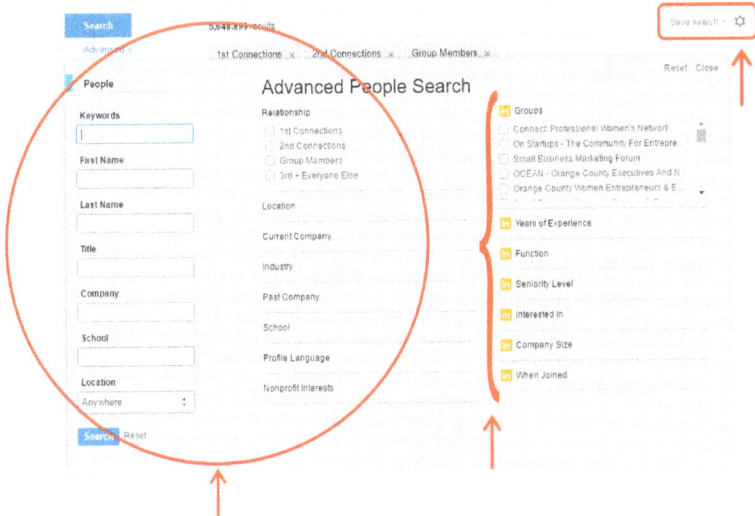

Not only do you have all these parameters to choose from; you also may save your searches.

For example, I typed "Trainers" into the keywords box and checked 1st Connections, meaning that LinkedIn will search my first-degree connections for people with the keyword *trainer*.

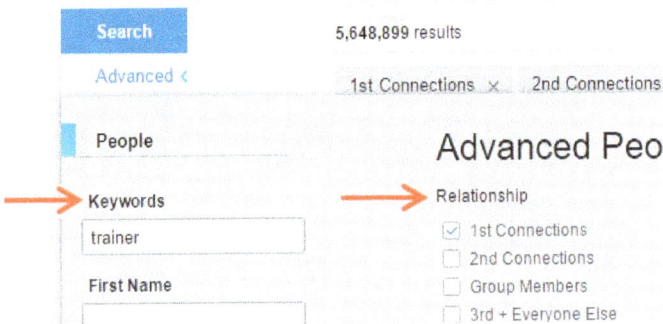

My search result was a list of all my first-degree connections with the keyword *trainer* anywhere in their profile.

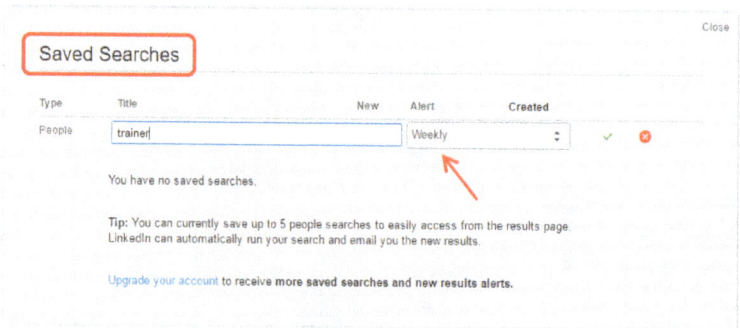

I then clicked Save Search in the upper-right corner of the page and landed on the Saved Searches page. Not only will LinkedIn save today's search for *trainers*, but I can also set it to alert me when anyone with that keyword becomes my first-degree connection within a week or a month (I can choose which) of my initial search.

CHAPTER 24

Long-Form Publishing

Long-form posts are meant to share expertise and insights. Each post you write becomes part of your profile, located in the area just above your Summary. When you're ready to write a new post, just click +Write a New Post in the upper-right corner of the Posts box.

You may also see how many people have viewed your posts and where they came from (Facebook, Twitter . . . whatever platform you shared the post on).

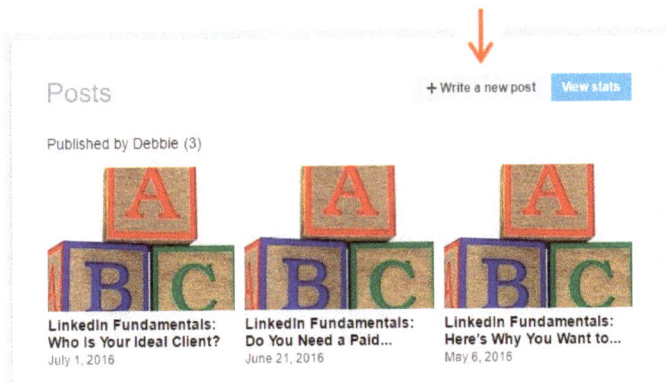

Once the privilege of Influencers only, everyone now has the ability to share their business insights, establish expertise in their field, and become a thought leader. Your posts will appear in the Status Updates section of your connections and followers. Even those you're not connected to can follow your posts and be notified when your next post is published.

Content can include advice, problem solving, how others can become successful the way you did, and so on.

CHAPTER 25

Conclusion

Thank you very much for your interest in this book. I hope I've achieved my goal of making LinkedIn easier for you to navigate.

Here's to your business success and prosperity on LinkedIn!

You can reach me the following ways:

- at my website: http://www.McCormickConsulting .BIZ
- on LinkedIn: http://www.LinkedIn.com/in/Debbie McCormick
- on Twitter: @McLinked

Neither Debbie McCormick nor Debbie McCormick Consulting is in any way connected to the LinkedIn Corporation.

This book is available on Amazon.com.

Appendix

Character Limits

1. First name: 20 characters; last name: 40 characters
2. Professional headline: 120 characters
3. Summary: 2000 characters
4. Recommendation: 3000 characters
5. LinkedIn publisher post headline: 100 characters
6. LinkedIn publisher post body: 40000 characters
7. Website anchor text: 30 characters
8. Website URL: 256 characters
9. Vanity URL: 29 characters after "www.LinkedIn.com/in/"
10. Position (at work) title: 100 characters
11. Position description: 200 characters minimum and 1000 characters maximum
12. Interests: 1000 characters
13. Additional info / advice for contacting: 2000 characters
14. Phone number: 25 characters[1]
15. IM (instant message): 25 characters[1]
16. Address: 1000 characters[1]
17. Skills: 80 characters per skill
18. Company name: 100 characters

---

1 Only first-degree connections can see this information.

19. LinkedIn Status Update: 600 characters[2]
20. LinkedIn message (InMail): 2000 characters
21. Group discussion title: 200 characters
22. Group discussion body: 2000 characters
23. Group discussion comments: 1000 characters

---

2 If you elect to also post your Status Update on Twitter, only the first 140 characters of your update will show on your Twitter post.